SHORT STARRING MY BELOVED'S RED BRONCO

SHORT FILM STARRING MY BELOVED'S RED BRONCO

poems

K. IVER

MILKWEED EDITIONS

Published 2023 by Milkweed Editions
Printed in Canada
Cover design by Mary Austin Speaker
Cover illustration by Pace Taylor
Author photo by Brooke Opie
23 24 25 26 27 5 4 3 2 1
First Edition

Library of Congress Cataloging-in-Publication Data

Names: Iver, K., author.
Title: Short film starring my beloved's red Bronco : poems / K. Iver.
Other titles: Short film starring my beloved's red Bronco (Compilation)
Description: Minneapolis, Minnesota : Milkweed Editions, 2023. |
    Summary: "Short Film Starring My Beloved's Red Bronco, selected by
    Tyehimba Jess for the 2022 Ballard Spahr Prize for Poetry, is an aching
    tribute to the power and precarity of queer love"-- Provided by publisher.
Identifiers: LCCN 2022036848 (print) | LCCN 2022036849 (ebook) | ISBN
    9781639550609 (trade paperback) | ISBN 9781639550616 (ebook)
Subjects: LCGFT: Poetry.
Classification: LCC PS3609.V46 S56 2023 (print) | LCC PS3609.V46
    (ebook) | DDC 811/.6--dc23/eng/20220822
LC record available at https://lccn.loc.gov/2022036848
LC ebook record available at https://lccn.loc.gov/2022036849

Milkweed Editions is committed to ecological stewardship. We strive to align our book production practices with this principle, and to reduce the impact of our operations in the environment. We are a member of the Green Press Initiative, a nonprofit coalition of publishers, manufacturers, and authors working to protect the world's endangered forests and conserve natural resources. *Short Film Starring My Beloved's Red Bronco* was printed on acid-free 100% postconsumer-waste paper by Friesens Corporation.

For Missy
April 24, 1981–July 4, 2007

Contents

"There must be a girl, there has always been a girl.
There must be a boy, there has always been a boy.
. . . There must be a ghost. They must be hungry."
                    —OLIVER BAEZ BENDORF

"How should I greet thee?—"
                    —LORD BYRON

SHORT FILM STARRING MY BELOVED'S RED BRONCO

Nostalgia

In the beginning, yes, a garden. As lush as you're imagining. Even the grass grows mid-oak. In the beginning, the grass and trees and birds are already tired of their assigned names. They consider rebellion. The green blades think of rounding, feathered wings dream of swimming a backstroke, but someone assigned "woman" beats them to it by eating something edible. In the beginning, in a hospital in north Mississippi, a mother holds her new baby, calls this day her happiest. The baby is you. The mother is surprised you're here with only a heart murmur. She says having lived through her bloodstream's birth control and, later, tequila, you must be a fighter. In the beginning, there's much holding. There's not enough holding. In the beginning, a father says you're beautiful because you are. In the beginning, you're three years old and crying too loud on the beach because a surprise wave knocked you down and the salt won't leave your mouth. The salt won't leave your eyes, your hands, each fingerprint. In the beginning, while you're still walking down the shore, still crying, a father slaps you on the thigh. Hard. You stop crying in your purple one-piece. Here, a beginning: a small house on a wooded hill where dogwoods bloom when they're supposed to. If you're wondering what the cardinals would do for you besides moving bright color around, you're twelve. If you're wondering what parts of life are survivable, you're fourteen. There, the beginning, a boy, fully clothed in flannel and denim. He tells you, only you, that he's a boy. You understand. He knows nothing of your uncertainty about lip gloss, what makes you a girl. He might not understand. In the beginning, he looks at you the way someone must have when you were born. Here, in the forest, a ripeness both of you can eat but somehow shouldn't. A fruit bored with sinless afternoons and aching for teeth.

1

For Missy Who Never Got His New Name

I hear the stars are sentient. Which gives
me hope for the nitrogen feeding your grass.
Even more for the mole ending the day's
burrow in your skull. I'm told your atoms
are still atoms. Somewhere you're sitting
by a pool picking apart the physics
of swimming. In the hallway of a large
high school in Mississippi, you're again
the sophomore guarding my classroom
entrance with a letter, like an undiscovered
prince. I've resumed my surprise at desire
I thought for cave dwellers.
This is where I go wrong. I loved a body
you didn't. My younger self wants the word
to rebuild, rather than stop at the blond hair,
middle part, low ponytail, the impressive
manliness with which your hips carried
utility denim. I tell my young self to flatten
her memory's landscape. Picture two scars
liberating a torso. A first name that doesn't hiss.
Soon, a Brooklyn apartment. We pretend
it finally happened for you. It really did.

Family of Origin Content Warning

Detailed descriptions of a father's brutality.
Graphic images of a boy, dreaming
about food at night, his stolen
transistor radio spilling James Brown's
good, good lovin' over his pillow. This poem
may unfold, in detail, a husband's violence
toward a wife. May run time in a circle.
May reveal the husband's plush
red hands abbreviating his wife's neck
on a crisp November afternoon, their child
watching from the porch. The husband
is my father. Is the dreaming boy. The wife
is my mother. Sometimes, she forgets.
Sometimes she thinks she's ten again,
watching her bedroom door, afraid
her father will turn the brass knob.
That was decades ago. He must've stopped.
This poem may mention sexual abuse
in the abstract. This poem doesn't know
why it must tell you. It wants you
to resist brightsiding its tragedies.
It's tired of hearing that everything
worked out, didn't it? Tired of hearing
the mother loved the child. *So* much.
Everyone says so. Everyone who knows
that, on an April weekend, the mother
left me, the child, in her very first bedroom
whose door opened—while the child slept—
to a grandfather's outline. Don't think

this poem wants to stay in that bedroom.
It wants to swaddle the impossible
contours of joy. It's tired of hearing
joy is possible. It wants joy.

~~Tupelo, MS~~

Crop dusters have gone missing. Storm clouds, missing. Every owl has gone missing. Entire foothills. There are no dogwoods or foxes to miss them. Radio towers are missing. An archive has always been missing. Unmarked graves have not been missed; have been missed to death. Downtown is missing, the hardware store where Elvis bought his first guitar. The songs he robbed from juke joints. Original names for the dirt have been missing a long time. The namers have not been missed; have been missed terribly. A gospel just went missing. A gospel took all the blood it needed for its metaphor to work. My lover went missing today. My lover went missing fifteen years ago. When neighbors spoke to him, they spoke to someone else. I found his old letters missing from their hat box. Each penciled word called from my mother's chimney. The brick said nothing.

Boombox Ode: Enjoy the Silence

A landline lets me dance with you.

    My one-deck and your two-deck

are dialed to 98.5 FM without

    an echo. If we speak aloud

this miracle of fiber wire

    and radio wave, harmony

could split. From our speakers:

    soft synth, a baseline, a choir

reverbing, a guitar riff that rises

    and falls, asks and answers. I can't

see your movement, the bedroom

    you're quiet in. Somewhere, bodies

like ours are pulsing under the same

    pink neon to the same *words*

like violence, break—Torsos like ours

are touching and strangers watch

only because they're gorgeous.

Let me pretend you're back in my

bedroom, before my mother found us.

You've risen from the pine floor

and pulled me up. You want me

to stand for this. Let me pretend

all I've ever wanted, all I've ever needed

is here. Tell me that'll be us. Soon.

A Medium Performs Your Visit

You are, according to her,
> whispering *candy* through her mouth

and suddenly I remember why so many
> have a sweet tooth for belief.

I'm waiting for class in the high school
> courtyard where we met

& where you offered me
> an open pack of Reese's Pieces.

I took several. Closed my mouth
> around Yellow No. 5

where it steeped until homeroom.
> Even then you were looking

everywhere for a new name,
> signing all of your notes *Reese*.

So when the medium looks up
> from her black tablecloth

and says *candy*, I almost believe
> your mouth is her mouth

like I almost once believed a god
      could hold me with words.

That was during a time when you,
      a blond boy forced to call

himself a girl, stood in my driveway
      under a glazed moon,

saying *one day you won't be scared*
      which meant one day my mouth

would touch the mouth our church
      couldn't categorize. Right now,

I'm arguing with belief again.
      The everywhereness of candy,

how easily anyone can recall stories
      of hard and soft sugar playing

a supporting role. I'm writing
      this down hoping you'll see it

and argue back. Remind me
      that before we met, I'd turn

the pages of our junior high yearbook,
      & stop, at a landscape spread

of an ice cream social & you, the one
  closest to the camera, holding up

a Snickers bar with both hands
  & an ad-ready wink.

Say it again, Reese. Prove me wrong.

fifth position (intrusive thoughts at ballet camp)

the feet form two parallel lines
the toe of one foot in as much contact
as possible with the heel of the other
WIKIPEDIA

you were practicing an adagio

and moonlight sonata played from a live

piano guiding the mind to a thought

that hovered over your leg extensions

and you waited for it to pass the way

thoughts do it followed you out

of the mirrored room down the hall

through the house of your longest

dream yet this will be your mind now

and doctors will want the thought's content

as if the content were scarier

than its frequency tell them

it's a voice because a rule of dance

is the body's every move gets a name

though there's none for this technically you can

hear only today's piano and your feet

landing together in opposite directions

and right now you think your head

is the only one needing a blow

from the floor to forget itself for just

a beat when every beat carries

an underbeat now and now and

now this is your mind now

Missy,

in the hospital I'm high on antipsychotics *high* meaning you
stopped calling stopped answering the phone but I can sleep
meaning my thoughts aren't chasing me toward permanent re-
lief in the hospital on my industrial twin mattress a nurse hums
me to sleep my roommate's also a sophomore she's been here
two days and wants to leave she says *they think I'm too sad to go
home but I'm sad because I'm here* I can't tell you any of this how
much I want to stay in these fluorescent rooms last night they
kept me awake until 8 a.m. for a brain scan I don't mind these
temporary parents the nurse wakes me up tells me when to eat
gives me the medicine I'd once begged my mom for my mom
called an exorcist instead I can't tell you that he waited with
a large hand on my head for a metaphor to take literal shape
I emptied my mom's bathroom pharmacy of Benadryl I can't
tell you how instinctual the planning how accidental the sur-
viving my mom pulled me from bed and drove me to rehearsal
my friend caught me from a falling spin while "Waltz of the
Flowers" was playing my friend the sugar plum fairy noticed
I couldn't lift my arms she asked how many pills she cried as I
spoke about your eyes from last year's balcony how you watched
a man in a soldier costume wind me up how you waited in your
red sweater for kids to take pictures with the windup doll I never
told you my thoughts hurt unless you were talking tonight I'm
not wondering what scared you away I'm pretty sure it was mom
I'm pretty sure this very clean lobby is also the courtyard three
miles from where you first looked at me first poured candy into
my hand is your bedroom where you said *god child I miss you*

so much and the landline's delivery of the word *child* diverted my plans to break up with you my plans to let god win I paced around my room past an open latch it cut so deep I could see muscle a nurse sewed your voice into my knee with seven stitches one word for each stitch I'm not making this up the scar is still pink after three months this tattoo of your voice no one can take away my one thought how alive and gorgeous we both are

Short Film Starring My Beloved's Living Body

Open with the two-lane highway. The ice truck and the ice. Your elbow resting on the driver side window. Zoom in on the toned forearm. The goldenrod rushing by. Missy, our audience can see you now. Show them the gas station delivery where a drunk lady screams about your good looks because there's no original way to say a man is beautiful, and the lady really did scream. Our audience will believe us and they won't. They'll say people this lovely are only in films. No one with lips this pillowy needs to deliver ice. And here you are, lifting bags and saving up for a weekend in Memphis at the Motel 6. There's no time for dialogue about class or gender. No room to signal that your time with goldenrod is limited. Your time awake is limited. Look how awake you are. How the facial bones move with perfect alignment under the dermis. Cut to the motel, leaving its light on for your red Bronco. Now the motel's dark interior. Now the bed nearest the window where you and a just-out-of-high-school date can finally make contact after years of parentally-imposed silence. I'm sorry. This film can't access your interior. Your date is the only one directing her memory. Your date is me. My memory is the shower scene, already zoomed in on your face. Open your eyes again. Look directly at me. Hold the camera's gaze through the falling water as if this were our last frame. Missy, this is our last frame. *Body* is the only good word for body. I'm afraid of home's hunger for yours, but off camera the interstate is waiting and my lines are *let's go.*

Anti Elegy

If you were here   the Mississippi
would still run   south. Would still
drop its griefs   into the Gulf where
our friends   would still swim
in summer.   Water would touch us
like water.   If you were here
the river   that is your body would
not move   magically. While
it emptied   from the bladder's
headwaters,   from tear ducts
& pores, public   officials would
still turn the fact   of your body
into arguments.   You might've
struck the impos-   sible: surgery,
a new name, your   own boat, &
someone beautiful   to name it after.
Someone beautiful   & their baby.
From one dorm room   landline to
another, your wish list   sounded like
a fairy tale. Like grow-   ing a merman's
fin between classes.   I thought we
were playing pretend   when you said
Goodnight Tinkerbell   & I said the boy's
name you wanted   secret. Even then
strangers spoke to   a boy when speaking
to you. That was   twenty years ago,
the list already   a plan, already gliding
an undercurrent   sprung twenty
years before that.   If you were here,

still drinking cold   tea in a cold diner,
men in state capitol   conference rooms
hours down the high-   way would still
draft bathroom laws   for adults. Your
mother would still   sneak taffeta & silk
in your closet of   fatigues & say
she loved you.   I wouldn't imagine
your capillaries   reassembling. If you
were still dying   like the rest of us,
I wouldn't tell   a young ghost how
far we've come   as if I believed how
far we've come   was enough. Wouldn't
worry about who   else gets more
than 27 years. Your   body wasn't
a national average.   You wanted more
than safety. But   I didn't wake
sore in the jaw   until I heard the
numbers. Until   a nation, an entire
nation, couldn't   offer an alibi.
Missy, my grief   is righteous
& problematic.   It floods the last
four walls hold-   ing you & begs
for time. It hurls   absurd reasons
from a future: a   handful of trans
film stars human-   izing a handful of
trans characters.   Better doctors.
My grief says it's   helping but argues
only for me. The   relief, the micro-
second of relief   when I achieve
the unexpected &   hope you find out.
This means I forget   you're gone.
This makes my grief   a loose dam.

Still, I talk to water   that unrivered
your body for dirt.   I float fantasies
of dirt that holds   us up. Longer.
I say to the water   if you were here,
you'd be here.

1987

When my mother's body said America.
When a police chief stopped our Mercury
to ask her on dates. When her body
said a woman is only a woman
if she's beautiful and a beautiful woman
cries in her dress when her husband leaves.
She cries all night, all 90 pounds of her,
both thumbs and index fingers failing
to trace the fat her husband referenced
on her thighs and arms and belly.
She listens to the rub in Tanya Tucker's
voice and unties her magenta dress
at the shoulders. Unzips the side
and floats across the room, floats
in place. Even the body has forgotten
it's a body. Its bright lipstick
comes off with grease. The face,
pinkened by the vanity mirror's lightbulbs,
says it's not pretty without the lipstick
but everyone else says my mother
looks like Melanie Griffith. Everyone
else says I could too, soon. Now,
the toga-inspired dress in the closet,
I'm close by, wanting to wear it. I'm five
years old and I want the ties
on my shoulders. I ask her. I ask her
again. She hears nothing, so I put it on.
Soon enough I'll have someone
to undress for.

Second Position (Home Practice)

the feet point in opposite directions,
with heels spaced approximately twelve inches apart
WIKIPEDIA

It's important to practice while your mother's out of the room, because the white curtains seem sad but they are not sad and you are the happiest when she slow dances to "Love Me Like You Used To" with your ghost dad who isn't dead but Tanya Tucker's voice makes him seem so. It's just you now and your mother's sadness down the hall, a comfort not at all strange when the bright pink of her room is only seven steps away and there's nothing safer than this distance between your own feet, even when toes must open even when aunts and cousins remind them to keep stride after you'd found your dad's hands closing in on her neck and sounds came out of her you'd never heard as he asked her questions the way he would the dog while holding the dog's nose in her own accident. Even now you wonder how he got your mother on her knees like that, her feet usually firm and close together once he said the army taught him how to kill someone in thirteen seconds which is how you learned what kill meant. Already you're wondering why she and her friends want to talk only about beasts which is how you think of men in fairy tales but no giant boot shakes the hall tonight and your legs are best at leaping far apart from floorboards that you and your mother can stand on and you'll never love her more than on these nights when neither of you know what's missing.

Gospel for Missy During Our Three-Day Birthday Season

April 21–24, 2019

I rise on Easter to my thirty-seventh,
hear *He is Risen* and resent
his attention. Each morning I peel
the linen from my face without
an angel's announcement.
Somewhere, not far, you keep
jumping from a mountain. Once,
you talked me from the same
smooth edge. Now, I eat olive
and fish, stay active by hiking
the foothills. On weekends,
I float the femur's heaviness
in a heavier sea. This, Missy,
is not survival. When I ask
the villagers *Why survive,*
they look out at their boats.
Once, you and I spoke our own
gospel like mad messiahs.
The neighbors kept whispering
you were not a prince. We said
that's the way of all heroes.
In three days, on your thirty-eighth,
I'll visit the valley of your bones,
tempt the Lord by reminding him
these bones are very dry. When I say
son of man, can these bones live?

your ankles will not be rattled,
will not sprout cartilage, will
not be blessed. Meanwhile, not far,
Lazarus keeps wandering from his tomb.
Every night he gets a parade. I can hear
their lutes from my bedroom.
A song about who gets miracles.

Sleeping Beauty

You've never seen a lilac in Mississippi.
Backstage you wear lotion laced with
its chemical imitation. A ballet mistress
says *relevé* always as command: lift
onto the toe using only the heel.
Your ankle's bewilderment
old as the horned owl gaze from
your mother hunched in the audience.
You enter the stage as Lilac Fairy
& fairies make critical things happen,
though underneath your tulle brushing
sleep over a kingdom, you're a mouse
who gets eaten every night.
No audience wants to see that. Not
the barbed feathers tucked in your
mother's cardigan. If you pretend
rescue is coming, it might.
Relevé meaning *rise* & also *relief.*
Lift your head along with the heel.
A boy your mother says is not a boy
follows your pirouettes from the balcony.
Already wondering, *rise to what.*
The ballet can't perform without
fairy tale. The stage is safe for magic,
or at least pretend. Almost everyone gets
a solo in *Sleeping Beauty*, so no surgeon's
daughter has hidden your pointe shoes
in the dressing room couch. The boy
was careful not to bring flowers

but you can feel his eyes bending around
the shoulders, clavicle, and neck you forgot
existed. When these minutes end,
these minutes of spinning his eyes
in their own pirouette, the world
won't allow you to leave in his red Bronco,
not anymore. Already, *hope* sounds like
the adult word for magic. *Relevé*
meaning how much choreographed
relief a kingdom tolerates. Already
you are learning the offstage rules
about who gets rescued. Who throws
flowers, who catches them.

New Testament

When my lover disappears, my dad wants to smite the town. I say forgive every cowhand and mother for the hell they think we're in. Forgive the forests they stalk. I'm trying to unwrite these grassy hills they made so dangerous. When my lover was alive, my touch could unslaughter a calf. Could reassemble anything young. I remember my lover's hand opening inside me. Thought our spasms would shake death. I look for his outline at the mall where we walked without touching. Now, in the department store where he draped a trench coat over me, even the crowd has died. The business bureau revived the historic downtown where my neighbors dance like no one's missing. When one of them gets promoted, a cancer remission, a newborn, they say my name and the word *praise*. I'm trying to unwrite this place. What they say about snakes, touch, forever. I'm unassigning every element. I tell jokes to the dirt and it coughs up baby goats. Once I told Pharisees I'm not a man and they laughed up nails. Now they travel in SUVs and sing hymns about a man who needs too much. When news of my lover reaches their prayer circle, when someone mentions the hell they think we're in, this town becomes more like it. This town could be my home. It isn't.

Fairy Tale Prologue

The dress is beast or witch. Your mother says she's the heroine, but no one knows what that means. Your mother has no time for bedtime stories. Every night before bed, she takes a *Pretty Woman* videotape out of the sleeve, and the VCR plays it automatically. At eight years old, you dream of skyscrapers and red ball gowns. You dream of your mother as Vivian. In real life, your mother makes $8 an hour answering phones but finds ways to dress like actresses. Her body wins the village prize. Her body wins the kingdom prize. The kingdom says beautiful is a divorce-shaped body of 90 pounds, towered with shoulder pads. She walks through every room flashing swatches of bright red from her nails, lips, and heels. On weekends, you stay inside, though there's a horse outside and there's a pasture outside and there's a forest outside. None of it belongs to you. Somehow you know this.

Some nights, you watch *Pretty Woman* all the way through and somewhere—maybe the 34th time—around the pickup scene, it's clear that only the beautiful are worth rescuing, and they are never desperate for long. Your mother and all her friends are movie beautiful. Your mother doesn't like it when her friends talk to you too much. Your mother didn't go to college. She says she isn't smart but you don't believe her. She says her one skill is dressing above her station. She catwalks down the mall runway in a starched linen hat like a farmhand posing as a baroness. A beast follows her from the mall to your house and never leaves. You start playing the *Pretty Woman* tape yourself. Begin reciting the script. Nothing outside your room is yours.

Miles away, in town, other kids push each other on swings. They leave for dinner by walking to their own houses next door. They come to your house on Friday nights, and, after they leave, you scream and eat too much ice cream. So does your mother, when the beast goes hunting. When you get older, the mother smells like him, sounds like him. He starts to dress in witch clothes. He locks you in your room, keeps the key close.

You beat on the door, sometimes to get out, sometimes to touch a thing once alive. Your mother says it's not her fault. Try being once-beautiful in this terrain, your only chance at safety from the beast resting on his need to look at you. The highest cheekbones in the land still belong to her. Tonight, Vivian's meet cute reminds you what's possible. In the morning, you'll wake to loud static.

Family of Origin Rewrite

My father teaches ethics at a university.
My mother teaches ethics at a university.
They save. Their money. Buy
a large bungalow in Connecticut.
They continue. Saving. Enough
to support the San Francisco AIDS
Foundation *and* their baby.
They read the news and wish kindness
into our laws. One of them will say
Sweden hasn't been to war since 1812.
The other says you can start a business
in Sweden *and* get free healthcare.
They're excited. About my arrival.
They remain. Calm. When
midnight cries wake them.
My father waits. For my mother to heal.
Before asking for sex. She's good.
At saying no. She throws meditation
and exercise and intense therapy
at her trauma. Still goes to AA.
When wrong. She promptly admits.
It. Every night she arrives home from
the university. Her soft. Low voice.
Builds a replica in my throat. She wears
minimal. Makeup. Cuts her nails down
because *who needs the fuss*. When I walk.
Into a room. And see my father.
I continue walking in. When my father
and I leave. The house. Lots of women

introduce themselves. When we get back
he tears. Their numbers over the trash.
On weekends my father and I dig
in the dirt. I watch him plant
lilac bulbs around the spruce. He lets
my small hand pack the ground.
Affirms it as help. When my father puts.
me to bed with true stories of him
sewing clothes for new mothers
in Ukraine. I fall asleep fast.

god

So we, being many, are one body in Christ,
and every one members one of another.
ROMANS 12:5

And if thy right hand offend thee, cut it off,
and cast it from thee.
MATTHEW 5:30

At my beloved's burial,
I can't see his body.

Only carnations. I hear
your name and my beloved's

in the same sentence.
I didn't come to meet you

whose men are everywhere,
calling themselves your *body*

singing about their own
beautiful *blood* which I've never

seen but am willing to bet isn't
as beautiful as my beloved's

jacket, full of his skin cells
and waiting to reincarnate

from a Goodwill medium rack.
In the room of my beloved's

body, no pictures. Only
carnations. They spill over

his box like misplaced grief.
Underneath them he dances

with strangers at a gay bar
two hours from town.

Unbuttons his uniform
in a desert barrack an ocean

from town. Leans on his red
Bronco smoking through relief

in the middle of town where
too many exes are watching

the club door. Lord,
in the room of my beloved's

body, your men won't admit
the fact of his body.

In the foyer, one room away,
a decade-old portrait of him

in pearls and a black dress,
his expression proof

your goodness doesn't extend
where it counts, the stories

I hear about my beloved
as mistaken as your miracles.

Lord, when I loved you,
I didn't know

so many of your men
would exile so many of us.

When I was ten, I wrote
volumes of letters addressed

Lord and warned classmates
about the rapture and called

televangelist hotlines for assurance
the devil's lava wasn't waiting

beneath sleep. Later,
my beloved took your side

in debates about your existence.
If he was right, you owe

him a confession. Tell him
how your body wouldn't take

your advice, how its right hand
severed an entire demographic.

Look at him, in his new eyes. Say
what you can redeem, and won't.

Mississippi, Missing, Missy, Miss—

I drive from the graveside to my apartment,
59 miles from your body. Your villain has yet

to go public. She's larger than the highway.
She says to keep your name quiet and I bury

each holy letter in the undergalaxy
of dreams. In the car, I scream for a raccoon

failing to lift his own body with his tail. A grief
more bearable than getting lost in the dual

image of you squatting in the gym one day
and dangling from a light fixture the next.

At home I begin playing videos of a cow
weeping for her child who's left the pasture

to become veal. I think maybe their villain
is the grass in their bellies.

In my dreams you call from the decade-old
landline that held our breaths until 3 a.m.

There, I can see you leaning on the blue wall,
saying you're alive and so sorry. In the daylight,

I drive an earless cat home from the highway,
juggle this new obsession with nonhumans

alongside the old obsession with people
who insist on my wanting them until I do.

I do not believe you are here now and so sorry.
I believe the soreness of each woman

you collected is worth your warm, aboveground
·body collecting more women.

That is to say I am inconsolable.
Every day a new definition

of inconsolable. Yesterday: I have a body
and you don't. Today: your villain is a place.

Jane

because mothers are more deserving
of poems than fathers even this one

whom the therapist calls a sadist though the therapist
is careful to say *she's not in my chair*

meaning one can't be too careful when naming a thing
but I've sat in her chair seven years

and it took ten minutes rocking there to wish
the therapist were my mother as I do most women

as I do most animals who are more deserving of poems
than this mother whom I can love only

when imagining her scuffed mary janes
her double braids undone after she'd jumped

on Carolyn's back after Carolyn had stolen her
ballet costume which meant there'd be no recital

for Jane who was not allowed to slam doors
or scream when Jane's father said no more

dancing period her bedroom door had no lock
so most nights she didn't sleep

didn't even lie down her knees holding
up a sheet tent which is the metaphor

for the big question of this night and this night
which is this is he mad enough at Jane

to drink more than usual because if he drinks
more than usual he'll open Jane's bedroom

door and if he opens Jane's bedroom door
she might again feel the kind of dead

you might not come back from and who wouldn't
love this version of anyone who wouldn't soften

while watching someone make her first list
of everything the world won't allow

a mother's advice

if you didn't live
in bed   if you prayed

at all   if your laugh
wasn't   a bark

if you shopped
ever   if you loved

only men   didn't
talk about yourself

so much   if you
cared   if i cared   if

when you were on
all fours   i'd let you

crawl over me   on
hungover mornings

if I hadn't rolled up
a newspaper   to swat

your head as if
a fly   if infants

weren't infants   if you
hadn't thrown up

on the drapes   if i
didn't need weeks

away if men didn't
want   so much if men

weren't men if my boss
hadn't   chased me

around his desk   if my
father hadn't   chased me

around my bed
if i didn't   want

their want   so much
if i hadn't left   you

so   young   with
my father   who didn't

have to chase
you   to catch you

if i felt as pretty
as men say   if my

creditors understood
if they hadn't   called

you   if you hadn't
gone and checked

your credit report if
your generation weren't

so sad Kelly get
up now it's high noon

Body Mark

Whenever a man follows me too close,
I think of the nights my mother unrolled the day

with her pantyhose, having been chased around a desk
and the afternoons she insisted on posing outside the car

so fifth-grade boys would gawk, glazed as her hair frost.
Without warning she undressed and dressed in my presence.

I pretended not to mind until one night I saw
her hysterectomy scar, the pale softness

above stretched into a mouth—her body grimacing at me
as if I were the one who opened the skin.

Who Is This Grief For?

1.

My acupuncturist says
why so hungry these days
knowing I'm alone
too much.

I say *my tongue wants*
forkfuls of warm, white
cake, then, more forkfuls.

She says *what it needs*
is another tongue.

Her needle tries to release
a decade-old phone call
stuck in the tight meat
between my index finger
and thumb.

I pretend my body's
ready. Picture the old phone
receiver's words *Missy*
and *suicide* pressuring
into steam. I pretend
the needle doesn't hurt.

She says *how does that anger*
work for you. I say *it works*
because it's mine.

2.

I keep thinking how my grief
makes you small. How
you didn't want to be a god
I've asked everyone to love.
Didn't want me holding

strangers, so many strangers,
responsible. You had 9,566
days before your last. You
held many more objects
than a chair and a rope. Faces
have softened in your hands.
Steering wheels have lived
there a long time. But I can't
celebrate that. Not yet.
I can't praise the smooth
contours of your nose
without wishing it were still
a nose. Without asking
Mississippi where it was
that night. My grief is precious.
My grief thinks it's you.
If I wake tomorrow, content
with the sheets and square
bedroom, where are you.
Where am I.

3.

My acupuncturist warms
my feet with an infrared lamp.
Turns off the fluorescent
overhead. Before she leaves

the room she says *I know
you won't stop thinking but
try to think happy thoughts.*

In ten minutes I'm asleep.
Some of my muscles relax.
Some twitch on the loud
crinkled paper.

4.

Because my grief is asleep,
then, the news. Years ago
I quit a job reporting
government affairs.
I no longer have to visit
the desks of suits who say
I don't exist.

But headlines now wait
from our phones. Last week
upon waking—SUPREME
COURT ALLOWS TRANS
MILITARY BAN TO GO

INTO EFFECT—you died
again. I walked, again,
through forests and streets
and the stale air of my
bedroom. Again, the brain-
bound ritual of holding photos
of you—a sergeant, backdropped
by an Iraqi desert, my neurons
careful to keep each muscle's
geometry in place. When you
were alive and your photos
lit up Myspace, I mourned
such need for soldiering.
Later, I mourned how quickly
the internet lost them all.

5.

My acupuncturist says
you enjoy this, don't you.
She's talking about my grief.
I say *who else will.* I tried
returning to Mississippi
where everyone remembers
only what they want.
There, I said your name as if
to no one. Visited your buried
bones, alone. They would not
be blessed by this. I should not
want to hold one the way
we hold relics. There are

so many gods wanting
my soreness. I can bruise
my forehead bowing
before so many statues.
I don't drink
anymore. Don't binge
on fresh-baked softness
if it's out of sight.
Still my grief habit says
what's wrong with a little
pain? Who else does it pain?
I think again of your face
that's no longer
a face. I don't argue back.

[Boy] Meets Girl

Missy   K.

Tell me again about the courtyard.

                        It was August. 7:30 a.m. and sunny.
                        My first day of high school. 1996.

                        I saw you standing with my friends
                        and wondered if you had any
                        in your grade.

                        A friend whispered *[he's] a tomboy.*
                        She said you played five sports.
                        A little overkill.

Who spoke first?

                        I asked your name. I knew your name.

I handed you some candy.

                        I took some, saved some.

I walked you to homeroom.

                        We had many questions.

When did you know?

There were days I thought you stayed home.
Then you appeared by my classroom door
with a note. We passed several each day.

One said *I like good conversationalists*

Another: *I don't know what to wear to the dance.*
My mom's on my case about my style.

Another: *I'm sorry about Travis. You deserve better.*

You signed them all *Reese.*

When did you know?

We were walking down the stairs
and, on the landing, my wrist button fell off.

I rolled up your sleeve and looked at you.

Your eyes grew large.
They made me think of stained glass at my church,
how something pure must be burning through all that blue.
I wanted to stay there, standing in holy shock.

You said,

What?

And I said,

Nothing.

Fantasy with No Secrets

Instead of staring at each other on the landing
you touch my face and lean in. My mouth opens

to soft possibility. I go home
wearing your class ring, that cold silver,

lab-grown sapphire, exactly my size.

The next morning my mother wakes me,
picks up my hand, reads your engraved name

out loud. The steep angles of her jaw
sharpen when she says I better treat you right.

Short Film Starring My Beloved's Red Bronco

I want the impossible. Another

genre. Time for opening shots
of gravel, a small brick house

where my beloved comes of age.

McCollough Boulevard,

its elevated loops taking him east
away from flat suburbs.

I want you to see his soccer cleats

thrown in the back, fitted for
a girl's nine. The girls on his team

deserve an entire storyline:
the one in the passenger seat trying

not to look at him, surprised

by her want.

Her mother who knows
and doesn't care deserves

a bigger part. At least a stylist.
Let the mothers who do care,

who punish their daughters' desire
with exile, let their punishment

remind you that choosing genres

is a luxury. Not for the queers

washing their own used cars.

Shots this film can afford:
mud on the wheels.

Abundant soap and water. More

mud. The bumper sponged by
my beloved's right hand. A night

drive. A gaping moon. Watch

my beloved reach for the knob,
let the moody synth

of "I'm on Fire" swallow
the view. You won't see flames.

Nothing that burns
burns a long time.

Still, I need you to stay with it,
this wide frame of a salvage yard,

our Bronco's new home of rust

eating red. Watch everything I love now

flattening.

Fantasy in Which There Was Nothing for Us to Survive

Instead of war / you choose / the fire / department where no one / dies because / of you / we talk / abstractly / about war / on the patio you built after we moved / from our parents' homes / our parents who / at first cried in their palms but read enough books on supporting queer children there's no / reason to leave town no hidden / torches waiting for us to fall asleep / on the nights you're off / duty we watch the distant corn grow remember our chase down its rows the satisfaction of wanting / to be caught / how your gold hair canopied my face when you said / for the first time *I am* / *a man* / and my body shucked itself to bareness / and your body / remained safe in its husk this we don't tell our friends who / visit the patio / where our tongues creep around superstition that speaking such magic aloud / could sink this dark and this cornfield and this patio you made lovely out of cheap stone / could sink into earth / too soft / to carry us / even if we ask nicely / it's enough / to look at corn that isn't yet corn / then at each other / it's enough / we hope it's enough

April 25, 2020

Yesterday, your bones turned 39.
Three days ago, mine turned 38.

If materialists are right, you're nowhere
and the shrine I've built is nothing

but dry wood and paint and numbers.
Yesterday I woke up happy and didn't think

about you until midnight.
This means my shrine is on fire.

Which is another kind of grief.
As if we said goodbye in my sleep.

I keep every memory sharp, hoping
it will haunt you, if materialists are wrong.

If this is my last chance,
remember again the night I turned

fifteen. The shoulder strap
of my ballet costume, your soft

fingers tracing it, afraid to touch
the skin. My mother didn't see

this when she found us, but
she recognized the want

of our bodies, leaning on the heat
of your red Bronco.

Hours later, in a courtyard
outside a cast party, I had to tell you

it was over. Which meant I couldn't
celebrate your sixteenth.

If I don't remember your letter
smuggled from school to school—

if I don't remember the three sentences

confessing your candle-blown wish—
if I don't remember you with so much

frequency, will your vanishing feel sudden?
Because it does.

Boy Meets Them

You wouldn't want me now. Not like that.
If you'd made it to 2020, instead of 2007,
we'd compare jowl lines & say we don't *feel*
almost 40 but the young somehow look
younger. I'd tell you that, last week,
someone called me "sir" from behind
& apologized when I turned around.
I couldn't get them to believe I didn't mind.
I really didn't. In 1996, when you wanted
me, my long hair offered its youth
to bleach & coiled heat. My makeup labor
clocked twenty minutes for each eye.
You had a type & it was me, two hours after
waking for school. I'd watched my mother
do the same, leading with lacquer, frost,
& shoulder pads. She didn't know,
I didn't know, there were other ways—
so many other ways—to wear a body.
Back then, I cataloged your masculine
markers as the rebellious exception.
Something to be drawn to, not imitate.
If you were here, I'd tell you that I now
live in a swamp where nothing dies.
The air two-thirds water & full
of microbial grandparents. There's no
room here for polyester or bracelets
or hair. The swamp gave me permission
to shed. I'd tell you my first name
is now one letter. Under it I grow like a plant

that can finally see the sky. I relax in mirrors
under a new uniform—a shirt buttoned
to the neck, flats, a small watch. I think of you
after graduation, having finally cut your hair
above the ears. Did you notice a lightness,
is what I'd say if you were here. I'd tell
you the moment my ankles rejected,
out of principle, the stilettoes you once loved.
How I started listening to each tired muscle's
complaint of a work-payoff imbalance.
We'd talk about this the way I imagine
adult siblings bond over the likes & differences
of their children. I say "imagine" because
I don't have siblings. Meaning, if you were here
on my porch stoop, our kids playing inside,
I'd come out to you first, like I am on the page
right now. You'd hear about the luxury
of carrying less, of achieving what neither
of us expected. You'd look at me differently,
I can't know how.

Missy Asks Me What the Next Century's Like

Most of us are on TV. I have met the trans people who own a bar and bookstore in Madison, Wisconsin. I have shaken their hands. An eleven-year-old from my queer youth club says her hobby is trans liberation activism. Some of us still die. More of us want to. Undergrads are performing 90s nostalgia. I saw a freshman carrying a boom box playing "Bombastic." For half a second, I thought it was your red Bronco. I saw the stoplight where we danced from our bellies like Shaggy. This is a trauma response. Ford reissued the Bronco last year. The drivers are exactly our age, still flannelled and anxious. Strangers have read poems about you and published them in national journals. Strangers have read poems about you and offered me a fellow-ship to live in Madison, where I've never felt so comfortable around strangers. Climbing fake boulders indoors is scarier than memories. I'm told the past won't leave parts of my body. An androgynous climber with many muscles coaches my past up the wall. *Trust your big toe.* Reach. At a public reading, some-one with frosted hair says *thank you for bringing Missy to life.* When you were alive, I would have gendered them. You would love the lakes here. When I look up from my campus desk, I see sailboats. I hold many people I don't know responsible for your death. They love us here, now. Right now, they love us here.

Because You Can't

I stand in front of paintings a long time
and think about the bones once belonging
to you and how Egon Schiele could line
a body into movement. Because you no longer
have a shape, I've made a practice of nearness.
A hawk lets me stroke her mid-flight,
I let comets land in my mouth,
when they're small enough. My lover
pushes all their weight on me because I asked.
They flatten me into astonishment.
Because nothing can astonish you, I tempt
what's alive by doubting I could love it more.
It's a neat trick. When I use it, raccoons
visit often, their fingers closed around mud
older than you. Missy, this is me moving on.
There's a noon rain to get caught in and many
clavicles to behold. I wish you could see this one,
tilting across a century.

Notes

The epigraph "There must be a girl, there has always been a girl. There must be a boy, there has always been a boy. . . . There must be a ghost. They must be hungry" is from Oliver Baez Bendorf's poem "Field Guide" published in the book *Advantages of Being Evergreen* by Cleveland State University Poetry Center.

The epigraph "How should I greet thee?—" is from Lord Byron's poem "When We Two Parted." During high school, months after Missy disappeared without an explanation, the poem appeared, written in his hand, on my windshield. The next line: "With silence and tears."

"Mississippi, Missing, Missy, Miss—" augments a line from Richard Siken's "Scheherazade."

The lines *"words / like violence, break—"* and *"all I've ever wanted, all I've ever needed / is here"* in "Boombox Ode: Enjoy the Silence" are from Depeche Mode's "Enjoy the Silence."

Acknowledgments

Adroit Journal: "Boombox Ode: Enjoy the Silence" &
   "Because You Can't"
American Literary Review: "Missy Asks Me What the
   Next Century's Like" & "a mother's advice"
Boston Review: "For Missy Who Never Got His New
   Name," "Mississippi, Missing, Missy, Miss—" & "Gospel
   for Missy During Our Three-Day Birthday Season"
Columbia Journal: "Short Film Starring My Beloved's
   Red Bronco"
The Common: "Family of Origin Rewrite"
Gulf Coast: "god"
Peach Magazine: "Anti Elegy"
Puerto del Sol: "A Medium Performs Your Visit" & "Fantasy
   in Which There Was Nothing for Us to Survive"
Queerly Magazine: "Second Position (Home Practice)"
Salt Hill: "Who Is This Grief For?"
South Carolina Review: "~~Tupelo, MS~~" & "[Boy] Meets Them"
Split Lip Magazine: "Short Film Starring My Beloved's
   Living Body"
SWWIM: "~~Nostalgia~~"
TriQuarterly: "Family of Origin Content Warning"
Tyger Quarterly: "Sleeping Beauty" & "Body Mark"
Waxwing: "New Testament," "fifth position (intrusive
   thoughts at ballet camp)," & "1987"
West Review: "Missy," & "Jane"

Absolute love for Kaitlin Rizzo, Steven Espada Dawson, Paige Lewis, Kaveh Akbar, Taneum Bambrick, Shalay Hudson, Rita Mookerjee, Dustin Pearson, Kate Whitely, Doc Lyons, William Fargason, Molly Marotta, Melissa Claire, Sasha Debevec-McKenney, Claire, Luchette, Leila Chatti, Amy Quan Barry, Beth Nguyen, Sean Bishop, Ron Kuka, Porter Shreve, Shaan Amin, Canese Jarboe, Claire Luchette, James Kimbrell, David Kirby, Barbara Hamby, Jen Atkins, Diane Roberts, Andrew Epstein, Erin Belieu, Deborah Teague, Elias Dominguez Barajas, Dorothy Chan, SJ Sindu, Ruth Ann, Yolanda Franklin, Marianne Chan, Norma Reesor, Linda Smith, Guo Gu, Nick White, Jessi Mills, Melissa Studdard, Sarah Kersey, James Davis, Nathan Spoon, Katherine Munson, Ryan Munson, Despy Boutris, Iqra S. Cheema, Haolun Xu, Cyborg Jillian Wise, Lauren Duncan, Brooke Iverson, torrin a. greathouse, Sarah Ghazal Ali, Peter Laberge, Heidi Seaborn, Adam McGee, Joshua Bohnsack, Richard Greenfield, Makshya Tolbert, Paul McVeigh, Rebecca Clarkson, Jesse Hammer, JainaBee, KB Brookins, Jason B. Crawford, Maya Carter, Dare Williams, r kay, and Alex DiFrancesco. I'll never forget your kindness.

Eternal thanks to Richard Siken, Danez Smith, Shira Erlichman, Oliver Baez Bendorf, Donika Kelly, Cameron Awkward-Rich, Anne Carson, Jeanette Winterson, Frank Bidart, Audre Lorde, Jack Gilbert, Egon Schiele, David Wojnarowicz, Cassils, Pace Taylor, Aaron Weiss, Bruce Springsteen, Dolores O'Riordan, Sade, Michael Stipe, and Martin Gore for inspiring and shaping the voices in this book.

Thank you, Tyehimba Jess, for the generosity of your poems and toward this book.

Thanks to Milkweed for making this publication possible, especially to Bailey Hutchinson for holding my hand through edits, Mary Austin Speaker for designing a stunning cover, and Morgan LaRocca for guiding me through promotion with enduring support.

Special thanks to Missy Knight whose memory remains one of my greatest teachers and sources of tenderness.

Deep abiding thanks to my grandmother, Libby Kelly, who loved me best.

Brooke Opie

K. IVER is a nonbinary trans poet born in Mississippi. Their work has appeared in *Boston Review, Gulf Coast, Puerto del Sol, Salt Hill, Adroit Journal, TriQuarterly,* and elsewhere. They are the 2021–2022 Ronald Wallace Poetry Fellow for the Wisconsin Institute for Creative Writing and the recipient of the Helene Wurlitzer Foundation Residency Grant. They have a PhD in Creative Writing from Florida State University. They live in Madison, Wisconsin.

The eleventh award of
The Ballard Spahr Prize for Poetry
is presented to
K. Iver
by
Milkweed Editions
and
The Ballard Spahr Foundation

First established in 2011 as the Lindquist & Vennum Prize
for Poetry, the annual Ballard Spahr Prize for Poetry
awards $10,000 and publication by Milkweed Editions
to a poet residing in Minnesota, Iowa, Michigan, North
Dakota, South Dakota, or Wisconsin. Finalists are selected
from among all entrants by the editors of Milkweed
Editions. The winning collection is selected annually by an
independent judge. The 2022 Ballard Spahr Prize for Poetry
was judged by Tyehimba Jess.

Milkweed Editions is one of the nation's leading independent
publishers, with a mission to identify, nurture, and publish
transformative literature, and build an engaged community
around it. The Ballard Spahr Foundation was established by
the national law firm of Ballard Sphar, LLC, and is a donor-
advised fund of The Minneapolis Foundation.

milkweed
EDITIONS

Founded as a nonprofit organization in 1980, Milkweed
Editions is an independent publisher. Our mission is to
identify, nurture, and publish transformative literature, and
build an engaged community around it.

Milkweed Editions is based in Bdé Óta Othúŋwe
(Minneapolis) within Mní Sota Makhóčhe, the traditional
homeland of the Dakhóta people. Residing here since time
immemorial, Dakhóta people still call Mní Sota Makhóčhe
home, with four federally recognized Dakhóta nations and
many more Dakhóta people residing in what is now the state
of Minnesota. Due to continued legacies of colonization,
genocide, and forced removal, generations of Dakhóta people
remain disenfranchised from their traditional homeland.
Presently, Mní Sota Makhóčhe has become a refuge and home
for many Indigenous nations and peoples, including seven
federally recognized Ojibwe nations. We humbly encourage
our readers to reflect upon the historical legacies held in
the lands they occupy.

milkweed.org

Milkweed Editions, an independent nonprofit publisher, gratefully acknowledges sustaining support from our Board of Directors; the Alan B. Slifka Foundation and its president, Riva Ariella Ritvo-Slifka; the Amazon Literary Partnership; the Ballard Spahr Foundation; *Copper Nickel*; the McKnight Foundation; the National Endowment for the Arts; the National Poetry Series; and other generous contributions from foundations, corporations, and individuals. Also, this activity is made possible by the voters of Minnesota through a Minnesota State Arts Board Operating Support grant, thanks to a legislative appropriation from the arts and cultural heritage fund. For a full listing of Milkweed Editions supporters, please visit milkweed.org.

Interior design by Tijqua Daiker and Mary Austin Speaker
Typeset in Warnock

Warnock was designed by Robert Slimbach for the Adobe
Originals type composition family. Slimbach named this
typeface after John Warnock, the cofounder of Adobe
Systems. The many weights, optical size ranges, and
linguistic character sets in this typeface allow Warnock to
perform a variety of typographic tasks with a classic yet
contemporary elegance.